My Favorite Business Quotes

Inspire, Motivate and Rekindle Your Fire of Imagination

EDITED BY RICK SEGEL, CSP

SPECIFIC HOUSE PUBLISHING
ORLANDO AND BOSTON

www.specifichouse.com

Published by
Specific House Publishing
268 Hamrick Drive
Kissimmee, FL 34759

© 2012 by Rick Segel

Requests for permission should be sent to:
Specific House Publishing
268 Hamrick Drive
Kissimmee, FL 34759
781-272-9995
800-814-7998
rick@ricksegel.com / www.ricksegel.com

Interior design by Julia Gignoux, Freedom Hill Design
Printed in the United States of America
ISBN: 978-1934683347

CONTENTS

DEDICATION

This book is dedicated to family because some of the best quotes come from family members. It might be a mother, father, uncle or grandparent that have favorite expressions, that they use over and over again. These expressions become our most memorable quotes and words we live by.

My grandfather, who I never met, had an expression that was repeated by his six children that made a lasting impression on me. He would talk about all the new changes that were taking place in America in the 1920s. He would constantly say with his Russian accent, "It's a new America." Those words apply even more today than they did then. That simple expression helps us cope and accept change.

Therefore, I dedicate this book to our family of unsung heroes that say the words that inspire generations.

INTRODUCTION

This collection of quotes has been painstakingly gathered by us for the sole purpose of providing food for thought and ideas for you to consider. These quotes appear in the Rick Segel & Associates weekly newsletter whose subscriber list is distributed worldwide in 40+ states and 19 countries. The weekly quote started off as a filler for the newsletter and then took on a life of its own. It is constantly receiving praise from our readers.

We hear constant requests from our readers for this collection. So for all of those who have been asking, this is for you! Please be our guest and use these in your newsletters, meetings, or signage as you see fit. They are meant to be shared.

I am frequently asked which is my favorite quote. The one I use the most, and that helps guide my decisions, is a quote from an unknown source that I use just about every day of my life. That quote is: "Let's not worry about the mule going blind, let's just load the wagon." We tend to worry about things that never happen—that only prevents us from getting the task at hand done.

My second favorite and most-used quote is a management philosophy from Michael LeBoeuf, a management consultant. He said,

The behavior that is rewarded is the
behavior that is repeated.

That sums up an entire semester of Management 101 in college. The last of my three favorite quotes is a simple expression from my mother-in-law that sums up a philosophy on living: "Busy people are happy people." Of course, there are hundreds of thousands of working mothers that might debate that point.

LUCK

I'm a great believer in luck,
and I find
the harder I work
the more I have of it.

THOMAS JEFFERSON

Hard work spotlights the character of people: some turn up their sleeves, some turn up their noses, and some don't turn up at all.

SAM EWING

That which we persist in doing becomes easier, not that the task itself has become easier, but that our ability to perform it has improved.

RALPH WALDO EMERSON

We play the hands of cards life gives us. And the worst hands can make us the best players.

DOC SEARLS

I say luck is when an opportunity comes
along, and you're prepared for it.
DENZEL WASHINGTON

Far and away the best prize that life offers
is the chance to work hard at work
worth doing.
THEODORE ROOSEVELT

Luck is what happens
when preparation meets opportunity.
SENECA

We often miss opportunity because it's
dressed in overalls and looks like work.
THOMAS A. EDISON

There are no secrets to success. It is the result of preparation, hard work, and learning from failure.

COLIN POWELL

Yesterday's home runs don't win today's games.

BABE RUTH

You make your own luck.

DAD

Learn to listen. Opportunity could be knocking at your door very softly.

FRANK TYGER

Chance favors only the prepared mind.
LOUIS PASTEUR

There is no royal, flower-strewn path to
success. And if there is, I have not found it.
For if I have accomplished anything in life, it
is because I have been willing to work hard.
C.J. WALKER

I feel that luck is preparation
meeting opportunity.
OPRAH WINFREY

Calm seas are beautiful for many but a
disappointment to sailors and surfers.
RICK SEGEL

It doesn't matter how many times you fail. It doesn't matter how many times you almost get it right. No one is going to know or care about your failures, and neither should you. All you have to do is learn from them and those around you because all that matters in business is that you get it right once. Then everyone can tell you how lucky you are.

MARK CUBAN

Integrity

"

If you don't have integrity,
you have nothing. You can't buy it.
You can have all the money in the world,
but if you are not a moral and ethical
person, you really have nothing.
HENRY KRAVIS

Good ideas are common—what's
uncommon are people who will work hard
enough to bring them about.
ASHLEIGH BRILLIANT

The keenest sorrow is to recognize ourselves
as the sole cause of all our adversities.
SOPHOCLES

When the character of a man is not clear to
you, look at his friends.
JAPANESE PROVERB

Try not to become a man of success but
rather to become a man of value.
ALBERT EINSTEIN

Nothing is a waste of time if you use the
experience wisely.
AUGUSTE RODIN

What we think or what we know or what we
believe is in the end of little consequence.
The only thing of consequence is what we do.
JOHN RUSKIN

Think like a man of action,
act like a man of thought.
HENRI BERGSON

I don't know the key to success, but the key
to failure is trying to please everybody.
BILL COSBY

Son, always tell the truth.
Then you'll never have to remember
what you said the last time.
SAM RAYBURN

Great minds discuss ideas. Average minds
discuss events. Small minds discuss people.
ELEANOR ROOSEVELT

If you think you acted stupidly you did.
RICK SEGEL

You can judge the character of others by
how they treat those who can do nothing to
them or for them.
MALCOLM FORBES

Greatness is more than potential. It is the execution of that potential. Beyond the raw talent. You need the appropriate training. You need the discipline. You need the inspiration. You need the drive.
ERIC A. BURNS

Lots of people want to ride with you in the limo, but what you want is someone who will take the bus with you when the limo breaks down.
OPRAH WINFREY

You have to have confidence in your ability, and then be tough enough to follow through.
ROSALYNN CARTER

There can be no happiness
if the things we believe in are different
from the things we do.
FREYA MADELINE STARK

On some positions,
cowardice asks the question, is it expedient?
And then expedience comes along and asks
the question, is it politic?
Vanity asks the question, is it popular?
Conscience asks the question, is it right?
There comes a time when one must take the
position that is neither safe, nor politic nor
popular, but he must do it because
conscience tells him it is right.
MARTIN LUTHER KING JR.

Everything people say isn't true. But we all
want to believe it is.
RICK SEGEL

Keep away from people who try to belittle your ambitions. Small people always do that, but the really great make you feel that you, too, can become great.

MARK TWAIN

In the end, you'll know which people really love you. They're the ones who see you for who you are and, no matter what, always find a way to be at your side.

RANDY K. MILHOLLAND

Nobody has things just as he would like them. The thing to do is to make a success with what material I have. It is a sheer waste of time and soulpower to imagine what I would do if things were different. They are not different.

DR. FRANK CRANE

People take different roads seeking fulfillment and happiness. Just because they're not on your road doesn't mean they've gotten lost.

H. JACKSON BROWNE JR.

Tact is the knack of making a point without making an enemy.

ISAAC NEWTON

We find comfort among those who agree with us—growth among those who don't.

FRANK CLARK

The difference between the impossible and the possible lies in a person's determination.

TOMMY LASORDA

There is scarcely anything in the world that some man cannot make a little worse, and sell a little more cheaply. The person who buys on price alone is this man's lawful prey.
JOHN RUSKIN

The greatest good you can do for another is not just share your riches, but to reveal to him his own.
BENJAMIN DISRAELI

There's only one way to succeed in anything and that is to give everything.
VINCE LOMBARDI

Life has no rehearsals, only performances.
ANONYMOUS

When you hire people that are smarter
than you are, you prove you are
smarter than they are.

R. H. GRANT

The true meaning of life is to plant trees,
under whose shade you do not expect to sit.

NELSON HENDERSON

It is not fair to ask of others what you are
unwilling to do yourself.

ELEANOR ROOSEVELT

I trust everyone: It's the devil within them
I don't trust.

FROM THE MOVIE *THE ITALIAN JOB*

Always bear in mind that your own
resolution to succeed is more important
than any one thing.
ABRAHAM LINCOLN

Getting ahead in a difficult profession
requires avid faith in yourself. That is why
some people with mediocre talent, but with
great inner drive, go much further than
people with vastly superior talent.
SOPHIA LOREN

Try to learn something about everything and
everything about something.
THOMAS HENRY HUXLEY

The only good is knowledge and the only
evil is ignorance.
SOCRATES

Better to light a candle than to curse the
darkness.
CHINESE PROVERB

Happiness is when what you think, what
you say, and what you do are in harmony.
MAHATMA GANDHI

Always render more and better service
than is expected of you,
no matter what your task may be.
OG MANDINO

Control your own destiny
or someone else will.
JACK WELCH

Handling criticism: if it's untrue, disregard
it. If it's unfair, keep from irritation. If it's
ignorant, smile. If it's justified, learn from it.
ANONYMOUS

Nothing in the world can take the place
of persistence. Talent will not; nothing
is more common than unsuccessful men
with talent. Genius will not; unrewarded
genius is almost a proverb. Education
will not; the world is full of educated
derelicts. Persistence and determination
alone are omnipotent.
CALVIN COOLIDGE

The mediocre teacher tells.
The good teacher explains.
The superior teacher demonstrates.
The great teacher inspires.
WILLIAM WARD

It's easy to make a buck. It's a lot tougher to
make a difference.
TOM BROKAW

Success is a journey, not a destination. The
doing is often more important than the
outcome.
ARTHUR ASHE

The only way around is through.
ROBERT FROST

Our lives begin to end the day we become
silent about things that matter.
MARTIN LUTHER KING JR.

A budget tells us what we can't afford, but it
doesn't keep us from buying it.
WILLIAM FEATHER

In prosperity, our friends know us; in
adversity, we know our friends.
JOHN CHURTON COLLINS

In essence, if we want to direct our lives, we
must take control of our consistent actions.
It's not what we do once in a while that
shapes our lives, but what we do consistently.
TONY ROBBINS

Follow the path of the unsafe, independent thinker. Expose your ideas to the dangers of controversy. Speak your mind and fear less the label of 'crackpot' than the stigma of conformity. And on issues that seem important to you, stand up and be counted at any cost.
THOMAS J. WATSON

Never trust the advice of a man in difficulties.
AESOP

Formal education will make you a living; self-education will make you a fortune.
JIM ROHN

The wise man puts himself last and finds
himself first.

LAO TZU

The desire of knowledge,
like the thirst for riches,
increases ever with the acquisition of it.

LAURENCE STERNE

Day by day, what you do is who you become.

HERACLITUS

Common sense is unfortunately not
common.

UNKNOWN

Money is only a tool.
It will take you wherever you wish, but it
will not replace you as the driver.
It is not the man who has too little, but the
man who craves more, that is poor.
Before you speak, listen.
Before you write, think.
Before you spend, earn.
Before you invest, investigate.
Before you criticize, wait.
Before you pray, forgive.
Before you quit, try.
Before you retire, save.
Before you die, give.
WILLIAM A. WARD

Leadership is doing what is right when no
one is watching.
GEORGE VAN VALKENBURG

Leadership is a potent combination of strategy and character. But if you must be without one, be without the strategy.

NORMAN SCHWARZKOPF

Let every man be respected as an individual and no man idolized.

ALBERT EINSTEIN

Life is just a series of experiences.

RICK SEGEL

To think is easy. To act is hard. But the hardest thing in the world is to act in accordance with
your thinking.

JOHANN WOLFGANG VON GOETHE

If there is such a thing as good leadership, it
is to give a good example.
INGVAR KAMPRAD

The greatest way to live with honor in this
world is to be what we pretend to be.
SOCRATES

The best vision is insight.
MALCOM S. FORBES

The expectations of life depend upon
diligence; the mechanic that would perfect
his work must first sharpen his tools.
CONFUCIUS

There ain't no free lunches in this country.
And don't go spending your whole life
commiserating that you got raw deals.
You've got to say, 'I think that if I keep
working at this and want it badly enough I
can have it.' It's called perseverance.
LEE IACOCCA

Let us not look back in anger or forward in
fear, but around in awareness.
JAMES THURBER

True intelligence is knowing what to say
when you don't know what to say.
RICK SEGEL

The noblest search is the
search for excellence.
LYNDON B. JOHNSON

The great leaders are like the best
conductors—they reach beyond the notes to
reach the magic in the players.
BLAINE LEE

To think creatively, we must be able to look
afresh at what we normally take for granted.
GEORGE KNELLER

To the degree we're not living our dreams;
our comfort zone has more control of us
than we have over ourselves.
PETER MCWILLIAMS

The enemy of the truth is very often not
the lie—deliberate, contrived, and
dishonest—but the myth—
persistent, persuasive, and unrealistic.
JOHN F. KENNEDY

Be the change that you
wish to see in the world.
MAHATMA GANDHI

The better work men do is always done
under stress and at great personal cost.
WILLIAM CARLOS WILLIAMS

I would rather lose in a cause that will
someday win, than win in a cause that will
someday lose!
WOODROW WILSON

We need to find the courage to say NO to the things and people that are not serving us if we want to rediscover ourselves and live our lives with authenticity.

BARBARA DE ANGELIS

In the realm of ideas everything depends on enthusiasm. In the real world all rests on perseverance.

JOHANN WOLFGANG VON GOETHE

You can buy a person's hands but you can't buy his heart. His heart is where his enthusiasm, his loyalty is.

STEPHEN COVEY

Avoid having your ego so close to your position that when your position falls, your ego goes with it.
COLIN POWELL

Good people do bad things and bad people can do good things.
RICK SEGEL

Don't bother just to be better than your contemporaries or predecessors. Try to be better than yourself.
WILLIAM FAULKNER

"

We cannot always build the future
for our youth, but we can build
our youth for the future.
FRANKLIN D. ROOSEVELT

Real heroes never brag about their
accomplishments.
RICK SEGEL

A man who makes quick decisions is
sometimes right.
FRANK MCHENNY HUBBARD

Dreams

"

The future belongs
to those who believe in
the beauty of their dreams.
ELEANOR ROOSEVELT

Live up to your potential
instead of imitating someone else's.
MARTHA BURGESS

You have got to discover you,
what you do, and trust it.
BARBRA STREISAND

Beautiful young people are accidents
of nature, but beautiful old people
are works of art.
ELEANOR ROOSEVELT

To want to be what one can be
is purpose in life.
CYNTHIA OZICK

Knowing others is intelligence;
knowing yourself is true wisdom.
LAO TZU

It's a funny thing about life;
if you refuse to accept anything but the best,
you very often get it.
W. SOMERSET MAUGHAM

Ability will never catch up
with the demand for it.
MALCOLM FORBES

All of our dreams can come true,
if we have the courage to pursue them.
WALT DISNEY

Life is like a combination lock; your job is to find the right numbers, in the right order, so you can have anything you want...
BRIAN TRACY

And in the end it's not the years in your life that count, it's the life in your years.
ABRAHAM LINCOLN

To accomplish great things, we must not only act, but also dream, not only plan, but also believe.
ANATOLE FRANCE

People rarely succeed unless they have fun in what they are doing.
DALE CARNEGIE

Never continue in a job you don't enjoy.
If you're happy in what you're doing,
you'll like yourself, you'll have inner peace.
And if you have that, along with physical
health, you will have had more success than
you could possibly have imagined.
JOHNNY CARSON

It's never too late to be
who you might have been.
GEORGE ELIOT

We are all inventors, each sailing out on a
voyage of discovery, guided each by a private
chart, of which there is no duplicate. The
world is all gates, all opportunities.
RALPH WALDO EMERSON

Lack of money is no obstacle. Lack of an idea is an obstacle.

KEN HAKUTA

The easiest thing in the world to be is you. The most difficult thing to be is what other people want you to be. Don't let them put you in that position.

LEO BUSCAGLIA

Plan your work, work on your plan, and your plan will work.

ANONYMOUS

The reward for conformity was that everyone liked you except yourself.

RITA MAE BROWN

If we all did the things we are capable of doing, we would literally astound ourselves.
THOMAS A. EDISON

Wanting to be someone you're not is a waste of the person you are.
KURT COBAIN

The starting point of great success in your life begins, in the simplest terms, when you discipline yourself to think and talk about only the things you want and refuse to think and talk about anything you don't want.
BRIAN TRACY

Do what you love and the money will follow.
MARSHA SINETAR

Do something. If it doesn't work, do something else. No idea is too crazy.
JIM HIGHTOWER

What is it that you like doing? If you don't like it, get out of it, because you'll be lousy at it. You don't have to stay with a job for the rest of your life, because if you don't like it you'll never be successful in it.
LEE IACOCCA

How am I going to live today in order to create the tomorrow I'm committed to?
ANTHONY ROBBINS

Do not be awe struck by other people and try to copy them. Nobody can be you as efficiently as you can.
NORMAN VINCENT PEALE

Don't give up on your dreams, or your
dreams will give up on you.
JOHN WOODEN

I have found that if you love life, life will
love you back.
ARTHUR RUBINSTEIN

You have to learn the rules of the game.
And then you have to play
better than anyone else.
ALBERT EINSTEIN

Your success in life will be in direct
proportion to what you do after you do
what you are expected to do.
BRIAN TRACY

There are two ways of meeting difficulties: you alter the difficulties, or you alter yourself to meet them.

PHYLLIS BATTOME

Live as if you were to die tomorrow…Learn as if you were to live forever.

MAHATMA GANDHI

Your time is limited, so don't waste it living someone else's life. Don't be trapped by dogma—which is living with the results of other people's thinking. Don't let the noise of other's opinions drown out your own inner voice. And most important, have the courage to follow your heart and intuition. They somehow already know what you truly want to become. Everything else is secondary.

STEVE JOBS

The road of someday leads
to a town of nowhere.
TONY ROBBINS

Twenty years from now you will be more
disappointed by the things that you didn't
do than by the ones you did do. So throw
off the bowlines. Sail away from the safe
harbour. Catch the trade winds in your sails.
Explore. Dream. Discover.
MARK TWAIN

The greater danger for most of us lies
not in setting our aim too high and falling
short; but in setting our aim too low,
and achieving our mark.
MICHELANGELO BUONARROTI

The main thing is to keep the main thing, the main thing.
STEPHEN COVEY

Put your seat belt on because the fun has just begun.
MICHAEL MANN

The worst days of those who enjoy what they do are better than the best days of those who don't.
JIM ROHN

It's kind of fun to do the impossible.
WALT DISNEY

You have brains in your head. You have feet in your shoes. You can steer yourself, any direction you choose.

DR. SEUSS

Life takes on meaning when you become motivated, set goals and charge after them in an unstoppable manner.

LES BROWN

When you really want to do something, the entire Universe conspires in helping you to achieve it.

PAULO COELHO, *THE ALCHEMIST*

High expectations are the key to everything.

SAM WALTON

Even if you're on the right track, you'll get run over if you just sit there.

WILL ROGERS

Imagination is everything. It is the preview of life's coming attractions.

ALBERT EINSTEIN

When nothing is sure, everything is possible.

MARGARET DRABBLE

The only limit to your impact is your imagination and commitment.

TONY ROBBINS

Do not follow where the path may lead. Go instead where there is no path and leave a trail.
RALPH WALDO EMERSON

If you can dream it, then you can achieve it. You will get all you want in life if you help enough other people get what they want.
ZIG ZIGLAR

I am here for a purpose and that purpose is to grow into a mountain, not to shrink to a grain of sand. Henceforth will I apply ALL my efforts to become the highest mountain of all and I will strain my potential until it cries for mercy.
OG MANDINO

We can change our lives. We can do, have, and be exactly what we wish.

TONY ROBBINS

The only limits are, as always, those of vision.

JAMES BROUGHTON

The difference between involvement and commitment is like ham and eggs. The chicken is involved; the pig is committed.

MARTINA NAVRATILOVA

Empty pockets never held anyone back. Only empty heads and empty hearts can do that.

NORMAN VINCENT PEALE

You can only become truly accomplished at something you love. Don't make money your goal. Instead, pursue the things you love doing, and then do them so well that people can't take their eyes off you.
MAYA ANGELOU

I had to make my own living and my own opportunity! But I made it! Don't sit down and wait for the opportunities to come. Get up and make them!
C.J. WALKER

Look well to this day. Yesterday is but a dream and tomorrow is only a vision. But today well lived makes every yesterday a dream of happiness and every tomorrow a vision of hope. Look well therefore to this day.
FRANCIS GRAY

The man who does not work for the love of work but only for money is likely to neither make money nor find much fun in life.
CHARLES M. SCHWAB

You must remain focused on your journey to greatness.
LES BROWN

Where there is an open mind, there will always be a frontier.
CHARLES F. KETTERING

You must either modify your dreams or magnify your skills.
JIM ROHN

The men who have succeeded are men who have chosen one line and stuck to it.
ANDREW CARNEGIE

Work is love made visible. And if you cannot work with love but only with distaste, it is better that you should leave your work and sit at the gate of the temple and take alms of those who work with joy.
KAHLIL GIBRAN

I wasn't satisfied just to earn a good living. I was looking to make a statement.
DONALD TRUMP

Why did I want to win?
Because I didn't want to lose!
MAX SCHMELLING

To succeed . . . You need to find something
to hold on to, something to motivate you,
something to inspire you.
TONY DORSETT

The bad news is time flies.
The good news is you're the pilot.
MICHAEL ALTHSULER

The beginning is the most important
part of the work.
PLATO

The creation of a thousand forests
is in one acorn.
RALPH WALDO EMERSON

We may need to solve problems not by removing the cause but by designing the way forward even if the cause remains in place.
EDWARD DE BONO

Everyone is a genius at least once a year. The real geniuses simply have their bright ideas closer together.
GEORG CHRISTOPH LICHTENBERG

Everyone rises to their level of incompetence.
LAURENCE J. PETER

Good business leaders create a vision, articulate the vision, passionately own the vision, and relentlessly drive it to completion.

JACK WELCH

Ambition is a dream with a V8 engine.

ELVIS PRESLEY

Humor

"

You cannot be mad
at somebody who makes you laugh —
it's as simple as that.

JAY LENO

Humor is also a way
of saying something serious.
T.S. ELIOT

Prejudice comes from jokes.
If you laugh, you are as bigoted as the
person telling the joke.
RICK SEGEL

A sense of humor is part of the art of
leadership, of getting along with people,
of getting things done.
DWIGHT D. EISENHOWER

If we couldn't laugh, we would all go insane.
JIMMY BUFFETT

Laughter gives us distance. It allows us to
step back from an event, deal with it and
then move on.
BOB NEWHART

To make a mistake is natural;
to stumble and fumble is commonplace.
To be able to laugh at yourself when you get
it wrong is real maturity.
ANONYMOUS

The funniest thing some people say is the
acknowledging that what they said is not
funny.
RICK SEGEL

"

Humor is the great thing, the saving thing.
The minute it crops up, all our irritations
and resentments slip away and a sunny
spirit takes their place.

MARK TWAIN

Laughter is the great social lubricant that
breaks down sales resistance.

RICK SEGEL

Humor is just another defense
against the universe.

MEL BROOKS

A joke is a very serious thing.

WINSTON CHURCHILL

The most wasted of all days
is one without laughter.
E.E. CUMMINGS

Look for humor everywhere—
its all around us.
RICK SEGEL

Like almost everyone who uses e-mail,
I receive a ton of spam every day.
Much of it offers to help me get out of debt
or get rich quick. It would be funny if it
weren't so exciting.
BILL GATES

Humor is reason gone mad.
GROUCHO MARX

In order to be funny
you must think funny . . . I think.
RICK SEGEL

A good sense of humor prevents the
hardening of the arteries and attitudes. It
keeps your joints and your opinions from
getting too rigid.
ANONYMOUS

The shortest line between
two people is laughter.
VICTOR BORGE

Everywhere is within walking distance
if you have the time.
STEVEN WRIGHT

A person without a sense of humor is like a
wagon without springs. It's jolted by every
pebble on the road.
HENRY WARD BEECHER

Analyzing humor is like dissecting a frog.
Few people are interested
and the frog dies of it.
E. B. WHITE

Being witty doesn't always work.
RICK SEGEL

Humor brings insight and tolerance.
Irony brings a deeper and less friendly
understanding.
AGNES REPPLIER

Humor is mankind's greatest blessing.
MARK TWAIN

Humor is something that thrives between man's aspirations and his limitations. There is more logic in humor than in anything else. Because, you see, humor is truth.
VICTOR BORGE

Start every day off with a smile and get it over with.
W. C. FIELDS

Success, Failure & Courage

Our greatest glory
is not in never falling,
but in rising every time we fall.
CONFUCIUS

If you don't risk anything you risk even more.
ERICA JONG

Success is not final, failure is not fatal: it is the courage to continue that counts.
WINSTON CHURCHHILL

Mistakes, obviously, show us what needs improving. Without mistakes, how would we know what we had to work on?
PETER MCWILLIAMS

Live in the past, die in the present.
BILL BELICHICK

We can forgive a child who is afraid of the
dark; the real tragedy of life is when men are
afraid of the light.
PLATO

Most people would rather be certain they're
miserable than risk being happy.
ROBERT ANTHONY

Our imagination is the only limit to what we
can hope to have in the future.
CHARLES F. KETTERING

You only live once—but if you work it right,
once is enough.
JOE E. LEWIS

Never regret. If it's good, it's wonderful. If it's bad, it's experience.
VICTORIA HOLT

Use your imagination not to scare yourself to death but to inspire yourself to life.
ADELE BROOKMAN

Enjoy life. This is not a dress rehearsal.
ANONYMOUS

Nobody got anywhere in the world by simply being content.
LOUIS L'AMOUR

Money was never a big motivation for me,
except as a way to keep score. The real
excitement is playing the game.
DONALD TRUMP

You always pass failure on the way to
success.
MICKEY ROONEY

Be not afraid of growing slowly,
be afraid only of standing still.
CHINESE PROVERB

It's not how many ideas you have, it's how
many ideas you make happen.
ANONYMOUS

Unconscious and incompetent means you don't know what to do and you have no idea how to do it. Unconscious and competent means you are a master.

RICK SEGEL

Waste not fresh tears over old griefs.

EURIPIDES

It is not the strongest of the species that survives, nor the most intelligent, but the one most responsive to change.

CHARLES DARWIN

Behold the turtle. He makes progress only when he sticks his neck out.

JAMES BRYANT CONANT

He who asks is a fool for five minutes, but
he who does not ask remains a fool forever.
CHINESE PROVERB

The important thing is not to stop
questioning.
ALBERT EINSTEIN

The policy of being too cautious is the
greatest risk of all.
JAWAHARLAL NEHRU

The only limit to our realization of
tomorrow will be our doubts of today.
FRANKLIN D. ROOSEVELT

One never knows what each day is going to bring. The important thing is to be open and ready for it.

HENRY MOORE

If you're never scared or embarrassed or hurt, it means you never take any chances.

JULIA SOREL

Why not go out on a limb? Isn't that where the fruit is?

FRANK SCULLY

If you can find a path with no obstacles, it probably doesn't lead anywhere.

FRANK A. CLARK

I would not waste my life in friction when it could be turned into momentum.
FRANCES WILLARD

The measure of success is not whether you have a tough problem to deal with, but whether it's the same problem you had last year.
JOHN FOSTER DULLES

Its not how many ideas you have its how many ideas you make happen.
COPY FROM AN INSURANCE COMPANY ADVERTISEMENT

Just do one thing better than everyone else.
RICK SEGEL

Here's to the crazy ones, the misfits, the rebels, the troublemakers, the round pegs in the square holes . . . the ones who see things differently—they're not fond of rules . . . You can quote them, disagree with them, glorify or vilify them, but the only thing you can't do is ignore them because they change things...they push the human race forward, and while some may see them as the crazy ones, we see genius, because the ones who are crazy enough to think that they can change the world, are the ones who do.

STEVE JOBS

Some people fold after making one timid request. They quit too soon. Keep asking until you find the answers. In sales there are usually four or five no's before you get a yes.

JACK CANFIELD

Each failure to sell will increase your
chances for success at your next attempt.
OG MANDINO

The way to get started is to
quit talking and begin doing.
WALT DISNEY

He who is not courageous enough to take
risks will accomplish nothing in life.
MUHAMMAD ALI

Success seems to be connected with action.
Successful people keep moving. They make
mistakes, but they don't quit.
CONRAD HILTON

There are risks and costs to a program of action. But they are far less than the long-range risks and costs of comfortable inaction.

JOHN F. KENNEDY

The successful person
makes a habit of doing what the failing person doesn't like to do.

THOMAS EDISON

If you do what you've always done, you'll get what you've always gotten.

TONY ROBBINS

I will not allow yesterday's success to lull me into today's complacency, for this is the great foundation of failure.
OG MANDINO

I dream, I test my dreams against my beliefs, I dare to take risks, and I execute my vision to make those dreams come true.
WALT DISNEY

Aim for success, not perfection. Never give up your right to be wrong, because then you will lose the ability to learn new things and move forward with your life.
DR. DAVID M. BURNS

When defeat comes, accept it as a signal that your plans are not sound, rebuild those plans, and set sail once more toward your coveted goal.
NAPOLEON HILL

Finish each day and be done with it. You have done what you could. Some blunders and absurdities no doubt crept in; forget them as soon as you can. Tomorrow is a new day; begin it well and serenely and with too high a spirit to be encumbered with your old nonsense.
RALPH WALDO EMERSON

Most of the things worth doing in the world had been declared impossible before they were done.
LOUIS D. BRANDEIS

Courage is the art of being the only one who
knows you're scared to death.
HAROLD WILSON

The only way of discovering the limits of the
possible is to venture a little way past
them…into the impossible.
ARTHUR C. CLARKE

It is hard to fail, but it is worse never to have
tried to succeed.
THEODORE ROOSEVELT

I have not failed. I've just found 10,000
ways that won't work.
THOMAS A. EDISON

If we don't change, we don't grow. If we don't grow, we aren't really living.

GAIL SHEEHY

The ability to be remarkable is dependent on the difficulty of the challenge.

RICK SEGEL

Don't wait until everything is just right. It will never be perfect. There will always be challenges, obstacles, and less than perfect conditions. So what. Get started now. With each step you take, you will grow stronger and stronger, more and more skilled, more and more self-confident, and more and more successful.

MARK VICTOR HANSEN

Sometimes when you innovate, you make mistakes. It is best to admit them quickly, and get on with improving your other innovations.
STEVE JOBS

Who begins too much accomplishes little.
GERMAN PROVERB

The majority of men meet with failure because of their lack of persistence in creating new plans to take the place of those which fail.
NAPOLEON HILL

100% of the shots you don't take don't go in.
WAYNE GRETZKY

All the adversity I've had in my life, all my troubles and obstacles, have strengthened me...You may not realize it when it happens, but a kick in the teeth may be the best thing in the world for you.
WALT DISNEY

Here is the secret of inspiration: Tell yourself that thousands and tens of thousands of people, not very intelligent and certainly no more intelligent than the rest of us, have mastered problems as difficult as those that now baffle you.
WILLIAM FEATHER

Surviving a failure gives you more self-confidence. Failures are great learning tools...but they must be kept to a minimum.
JEFFREY IMMELT

The important thing is not being afraid to take a chance. Remember, the greatest failure is to not try. Once you find something you love to do, be the best at doing it.
DEBBI FIELDS

Every accomplishment starts with the decision to try.
ANONYMOUS

We generate fears while we sit. We overcome them by action. Fear is nature's way of warning us to get busy.
DR. HENRY LINK

A big part of financial freedom is having your heart and mind free from worry about the what-ifs of life.

SUZE ORMAN

Victory is sweetest when you've known defeat.

MALCOLM FORBES

Falling down is how we grow. Staying down is how we die.

BRIAN VASZILY

Life is like riding a bicycle. To keep your balance, you must keep moving.

ALBERT EINSTEIN

People who don't take risks generally make about two big mistakes a year. People who do take risks generally make about two big mistakes a year.
PETER F. DRUCKER

If you do not know how to ask the right question, you discover nothing.
WILLIAM EDWARDS DEMING

If you don't go after what you want, you'll never have it. If you don't ask, the answer is always no. If you don't step forward, you're always in the same place.
NORA ROBERTS

Only those who will risk going too far can
possibly find out how far one can go.

T. S. ELIOT

It's fine to celebrate success but it is more
important to heed the lessons of failure.

BILL GATES

Live daringly, boldly, fearlessly. Taste the
relish to be found in competition—in having
put forth the best within you.

HENRY J. KAISER

You only have to do a very few things right
in your life so long as you don't do too many
things wrong.

WARREN BUFFETT

To win without risk
is to triumph without glory.
PIERRE CORNEILLE

Winners take time to relish their work,
knowing that scaling the mountain is what
makes the view from the top so exhilarating.
DENIS WAITLEY

The most serious mistakes are not being
made as a result of wrong answers. The truly
dangerous thing is asking the wrong
question.
PETER F. DRUCKER

If a man will begin with certainties, he shall
end in doubts; but if he will be content to
begin with doubts, he shall end in certainty.
FRANCIS BACON

Failure is the foundation of success; success
is the lurking place of failure.
LAO TZU

There can be no hope without fear, and no
fear without hope.
BARUCH SPINOZA

Whenever you see a successful business,
someone once made a courageous decision.
PETER F. DRUCKER

Success is often achieved by those who don't
know that failure is inevitable.
COCO CHANEL

Many great ideas go unexecuted, and many
great executioners are without ideas. One
without the other is worthless.
TIM BLIXSETH

The wheel that squeaks the loudest is the
one that gets the grease.
JOSH BILLINGS

Our favorite holding period is forever.
WARREN BUFFETT

Obstacles don't have to stop you. If you run into a wall, don't turn around and give up. Figure out how to climb it, go through it, or work around it.

MICHAEL JORDAN

The rule is simple . . . you do it today! One finds limits by pushing them.

HERBERT SIMON

Big shots are just little shots that keep shooting.

CHRISTOPHER MORLEY

Every failure brings you closer to success.

RICK SEGEL

You learn to speak by speaking, to study by
studying, to run by running, to work by
working; and just so, you learn to love by
loving. All those who think to learn in any
other way deceive themselves.
ANATOLE FRANCE

I could have been a contender.
ON THE WATER FRONT, MARLON BRANDO

Okay, Houston, we've had a problem here.
APOLLO 13 MISSION, JOHN SWIGERT, JR

Failure is not an option.
MOVIE APOLLO 13, ED HARRIS

The difference between winning and losing is so small it's a shame we call the ones that don't win losers.

RICK SEGEL

We are never as great as our greatest victory or as bad as our worst defeat.

DR. ALAN WEISS

The thrill of victory and the agony of defeat.

ABC SPORTS INTRO

The more information you have about a topic the better the decision should be.

RICK SEGEL

Great men are rarely isolated mountain
peaks; they are the summits of ranges.
THOMAS W. HIGGINSON

When the horse is DEAD get off of it.
ROBIN L. SILVERMAN

Success is not final, failure is not fatal:
it is the courage to continue that counts.
WINSTON CHURCHILL

Mistakes are always forgivable, if one has the
courage to admit them.
BRUCE LEE

One man with courage is a majority.
THOMAS JEFFERSON

We must build dikes of courage to hold back
the flood of fear.
MARTIN LUTHER KING, JR.

Constant never-ending improvements keep a
business and people alive and well.
RICK SEGEL

Kindness

I've learned that
people will forget what you said,
people will forget what you did,
but people will never forget
how you made them feel.
MAYA ANGELOU

If you make it plain you like people, it's hard
for them to resist liking you back.
LOIS MCMASTER BUJOLD

Make all you can, save all you can,
give all you can.
JOHN WESLEY

Do not forget small kindnesses
and do not remember small faults.
CHINESE PROVERB

A life is not important except in
the impact it has on other lives.
JACKIE ROBINSON

Be kind, for everyone you meet is fighting a
harder battle.
PLATO

Is the rich world aware of how
four billion of the six billion live?
If we were aware, we would want to help
out, we'd want to get involved.
BILL GATES

Beginning today, treat everyone you meet as
if they were going to be dead by midnight.
Extend them all the care, kindness and
understanding you can muster. Your life will
never be the same again.
OG MANDINO

Guard well within yourself that treasure, kindness. Know how to give without hesitation, how to lose without regret, how to acquire without meanness.

GEORGE SAND

Capturing the profound words we speak is like trying to catch a butterfly.

RICK SEGEL

Kind words can be short and easy to speak, but their echoes are truly endless.

MOTHER TERESA

Kindness is a language which the deaf can hear and the blind can see.

MARK TWAIN

You cannot do a kindness too soon, for you never know how soon it will be too late.
RALPH WALDO EMERSON

No one has ever become poor by giving.
ANNE FRANK, *DIARY OF ANNE FRANK*

But remember, boy, that a kind act can sometimes be as powerful as a sword.
RICK RIORDAN, *THE BATTLE OF THE LABYRINTH*

Never look down on anybody unless you're helping them up.
JESSE JACKSON

The test of our progress is not whether we add more to the abundance of those who have much; it is whether we provide enough for those who have too little.

FRANKLIN D. ROOSEVELT

There is nothing so rewarding as to make people realize that they are worthwhile in this world.

BOB ANDERSON

A kind word is like a Spring day.

RUSSIAN PROVERB

One can pay back the loan of gold, but one dies forever in debt to those who are kind.

MALAYAN PROVERB

If you haven't any charity in your heart, you have the worst kind of heart trouble.

BOB HOPE

The best way to knock the chip off your neighbor's shoulder is to pat him on the back.

AUTHOR UNKNOWN

I always prefer to believe the best of everybody, it saves so much trouble.

RUDYARD KIPLING

Real charity doesn't care
if it's tax-deductible or not.

DAN BENNETT

Kindness is in our power,
even when fondness is not.
SAMUEL JOHNSON

The most important trip you may take in life
is meeting people halfway.
HENRY BOYE

Getting money is not all a man's business:
to cultivate kindness is a valuable part
of the business of life.
SAMUEL JOHNSON

When I was young, I admired clever people.
Now that I am old, I admire kind people.
ABRAHAM JOSHUA HESCHEL

The true meaning of life is to plant trees,
under whose shade you do not expect to sit.
NELSON HENDERSON

A mistake made by many people with great
convictions is that they will let nothing
stand in the way of their views, not even
kindness.
BRYANT H. MCGILL

A warm smile is the universal language of
kindness.
WILLIAM ARTHUR WARD

The greatest good you can do for another is
not just to share your riches but to reveal to
him his own.
BENJAMIN DISRAELI

Industry, economy, honesty, and kindness form a quartet of virtues that will never be improved upon.

JAMES OLIVER

He that has done you a kindness will be more ready to do you another, than he whom you yourself have obliged.

BENJAMIN FRANKLIN

Constant kindness can accomplish much. As the sun makes ice melt, kindness causes misunderstanding, mistrust, and hostility to evaporate.

ALBERT SCHWEITZER

Consensus means no one wins.

RICK SEGEL

A little thought and a little kindness are often worth more than a great deal of money.
JOHN RUSKIN

Real generosity is doing something nice for someone who will never find out.
FRANK A. CLARK

Constant kindness can accomplish much. As the sun makes ice melt, kindness causes misunderstanding, mistrust, and hostility to evaporate.
ALBERT SCHWEITZER:

The greatest work that kindness does to others is that it makes them kind themselves.
AMELIA EARHART

The only way to tell the truth is to speak with kindness. Only the words of a loving man can be heard.

HENRY DAVID THOREAU

Three things in human life are important. The first is to be kind. The second is to be kind. The third is to be kind.

HENRY JAMES

Life is not so short but that there is always time enough for courtesy.

RALPH WALDO EMERSON

Attitude

"

The mind is everything.
What you think, you become.
BUDDHA

Life may not be the party we hoped for, but
while we are here we might as well dance.
ANONYMOUS

Even with the best of maps and instruments,
we can never fully chart our journeys.
GAIL POOL

Pick battles big enough to matter, small
enough to win.
JONATHAN KOZOL

A rich man is nothing more than a poor man
with money.
W.C. FIELDS

Motivation comes from within.
RICK SEGEL

It takes no more time to see the good side of
life than to see the bad.
JIMMY BUFFETT

Think little goals and expect little
achievements. Think big goals and win big
success.
DAVID JOSEPH SCHWARTZ

Focus 90% of your time on solutions and
only 10% of your time on problems.
ANTHONY J. D'ANGELO

The greatest discovery of my generation is that a human being can alter his life by altering his attitudes of mind.
WILLIAM JAMES

The optimist sees the rose and not its thorns; the pessimist stares at the thorns, oblivious of the rose.
KAHLIL GIBRAN

That some should be rich, shows that others may become rich, and, hence, is just encouragement to industry and enterprise.
ABRAHAM LINCOLN

You're gonna need a bigger boat.
JAWS, ROY SCHEIDER

We always like those who admire us; we do
not always like those whom we admire.
FRANÇOIS DE LA ROCHEFOUCAULD

Not to know is bad.
Not to wish to know is worse.
AFRICAN PROVERB

Never, never rest contented with any circle
of ideas, but always be certain that a wider
one is still possible.
PEARL BAILEY

A strong positive mental attitude will create
more miracles than any wonder drug.
PATRICIA NEAL

Winning isn't everything—
but wanting to win is.
VINCE LOMBARDI

When it comes to life the critical thing is
whether you take things for granted or take
them with gratitude.
GILBERT KEITH CHESTERSON

Take the attitude of a student, never be too
big to ask questions, never know too much
to learn something new.
OG MANDINO

The minute you start thinking that you've
done it all, that's when you're in the rear
view mirror.
CHRIS DEWOLFE

Winning is not everything,
but the effort to win is.
ZIG ZIGLAR

The winners in life think constantly in terms
of I can, I will, and I am. Losers, on the
other hand, concentrate their waking
thoughts on what they should have or
would have done, or what they can't do.
DENNIS WAITLEY

The more aggravated you are the less
effective you become.
RICK SEGEL

Ninety percent of the game is half mental.
YOGI BERRA

The trick is in what one emphasizes. We either make ourselves miserable, or we make ourselves strong. The amount of work is the same.

CARLOS CASTANEDA

Whatever the mind can conceive and believe, it can achieve. Thoughts are things! And powerful things at that, when mixed with definiteness of purpose, and burning desire, can be translated into riches.

NAPOLEON HILL

Nothing great was ever achieved without enthusiasm.

RALPH WALDO EMERSON

Always make the other guy more important.
RICK SEGEL

People often say motivation don't last. Well,
neither does bathing. That's why we
recommend it daily!
ZIG ZIGLAR

Everything should be made as simple as
possible, but not simpler.
ALBERT EINSTEIN

There is no security on this earth,
there is only opportunity.
GENERAL DOUGLAS MACARTHUR

If you think you can, you can. And if you think you can't, you're right.
MARY KAY ASH

If you don't look up to see the tops of the tall buildings because you think you will look like a tourist, ask yourself, what is wrong with acting like a tourist?
RICK SEGEL

Do or do not. There is no try.
YODA

Confidence is contagious.
So is lack of confidence.
VINCE LOMBARDI

Don't tell me the sky's the limit when there are footprints on the moon!
ANONYMOUS

Inspiration exists, but it has to find you working.
PABLO PICASSO

As long as you're going to be thinking anyway, think big!
DONALD TRUMP

When dealing with an emotionally upset person be prepared to take the blame for something.
RICK SEGEL

It's not what happens to you, it's what you
do with what happens to you.
ALDOUS HUXLEY

The eyes go where the car goes.
THE ART OF RACING IN THE RAIN

In order to succeed, we must first believe
that we can.
NIKOS KAZANTZAKIS

How you think when you lose determines
how long it will be until you win.
GILBERT KEITH CHESTERTON

As you travel down life's highway . . .
whatever be your goal, you cannot sell a
doughnut without acknowledging the hole.
HAROLD J. SHAYLER

I never looked at the consequences of
missing a big shot . . . when you think about
the consequences you always think of a
negative result.
MICHAEL JORDAN

Happiness is not in the mere possession of
money; it lies in the joy of achievement, in
the thrill of creative effort.
FRANKLIN D. ROOSEVELT

The good or ill of a man lies within his own will.
EPICTETUS

The customer is NOT always RIGHT but they are the customer and they are allowed to make a mistake.
RICK SEGEL

The cynic says, 'One man can't do anything.'
I say, 'Only one man can do anything.'
JOHN W. GARDNER

The great accomplishments of man have resulted from the transmission of ideas of enthusiasm.
THOMAS J. WATSON

The believer is happy;
the doubter is wise.
HUNGARIAN PROVERB

The best is yet to be.
ROBERT BROWNING

The best thing about the future is that it
only comes one day at a time.
ABRAHAM LINCOLN

Whether you think you can or whether you
think you can't, you're right!
HENRY FORD

We cannot direct the wind, but we can
adjust the sails.
BERTHA CALLOWAY

It is not what happens to you, it is what you
do about it.
W. MITCHELL

Slump? I ain't in no slump.
I just ain't hittin'.
YOGI BERRA

If you think you are at the end of your
strength you have another 10% left.
RICK SEGEL

The first and most important step toward
success is the feeling that we can succeed.
NELSON BOSWELL

Success is a state of mind. If you want
success, start thinking of yourself as a
success.
DR. JOYCE BROTHERS

We would accomplish many more things if
we did not think of them as impossible.
VINCE LOMBARDI

Most folks are about as happy as they make
up their minds to be.
ABRAHAM LINCOLN

You are surrounded by simple, obvious solutions that can dramatically increase your income, power, influence and success. The problem is, you just don't see them.

JAY ABRAHAM

Winning is not a sometime thing; it's an all-time thing. You don't win once in a while, you don't do things right once in a while, you do them right all the time. Winning is habit. Unfortunately, so is losing

VINCE LOMBARDI

Intimidation is a very powerful tool employed by many.

RICK SEGEL

We can learn from a fool.
RICK SEGEL

Your job is to ask, How could we do it
better? How could we do it cheap? Or How
else do we do it?
BEN KROFCHAK

Take a big bite out of life,
so what if some stuff falls out.
RICK SEGEL

Let's agree to disagree.
UNKNOWN

Make it fun and customers will come.
RICK SEGEL

Ask what you can do for your wife not what
your wife can do for you.
UNKNOWN

You can't handle the truth.
.A FEW GOOD MEN, JACK NICHOLSON

The art of persuasion is letting the other
person think they are getting their way when
they are not.
UNKNOWN

It is what it is.
TOM ROBBINS

You talkin' to me?
TAXI DRIVER, ROBERT DE NIRO

I'm mad as hell and I am not going to take it
anymore.
NETWORK, PETER FINCH

Having someone try something new can be
as frustrating as training a cat.
RICK SEGEL

If you build it, they will come.
FIELD OF DREAMS

Life is like a box of chocolates, you never
know what you are going to get.
FORREST GUMP, TOM HANKS

Frankly scarlet, I don't give a damn.
GONE WITH THE WIND, CARY GRANT

I skate to where the puck is going to be not
to where it's been.
WAYNE GRETSKI

I'll take enthusiasm over almost
any other business trait.
RICK SEGEL

Hire attitude, train skills.
UNKNOWN

Choose a job that you like and you will
never have to work a day in your life.
CONFUCIUS

It is easier to beg forgiveness
than to ask permission.
UNKNOWN

Everyone must believe that the customer is the key to the business and we are willing to do whatever it takes to impress them.

RICK SEGEL

There's no crying in baseball.

A LEAGUE OF THEIR OWN, TOM HANKS

Business

If you don't drive your business,
you will be driven out of business.
B.C. FORBES

It is impossible to tell the customer no and
have the customer thank you for doing it.
PHIL KNIGHT

If everything is always on sale
where is the sale?
RICK SEGEL

Sell crazy someplace else,
we're all stocked up here.
AS GOOD AS IT GETS, JACK NICHOLSON

What we have here is a failure to
communicate.
COOL HAND LUKE, STROTHER MARTIN

Good design can fix
a broken business model.
RICK SEGEL

I'm gonna make him an offer he can't refuse.
THE GODFATHER, MARLIN BRANDO

Don't be irreplaceable, if you can't be
replaced you can't be promoted.
MURPHY'S LAW

A bad reference is as hard to find as a good
employee.
ROBERT HALF

When we finish one product-development program, we raise our heads and look around to see what to invent next.

ED MCCRACKEN

If you want to find out what a company is doing don't listen to the security analyst, they talk profit, which is irrelevant. Listen to Bak credit analysts, they talk cash flow.

WARREN BUFFET

Be careful of the paralysis of analysis when information overloads the decision process.

RICK SEGEL

The guy with competitive advantage is the
one with the best technology.
WALT WRISTON

Before we gotta make a decision, make sure
it makes sense.
UNKNOWN

Economists have the best job in the world. If
they're right they're heros, if the are wrong
they have built in excuses.
RICK SEGEL

There is nothing so horrible in nature to see
a beautiful theory, murdered by an
ugly gang of facts.
BEN FRANKLIN

Don't open a shop unless you like to smile.
CHINESE PROVERB

Profit in business comes from repeat customers, customers that boast about your project or service, and that bring friends with them.
W. EDWARDS DEMING

There is only one boss. The customer. And he can fire everybody in the company from the chairman on down, simply by spending his money somewhere else.
SAM WALTON

Trends are just fads that refuse to go away.
RICK SEGEL

"

You can't do today's job with yesterday's methods and be in business tomorrow.
ANONYMOUS

Look at your business the way front line people do and you will always have the customer's perspective in mind.
RICK SEGEL

I've never felt like I was in the cookie business. I've always been in a feel-good feeling business. My job is to sell joy. My job is to sell happiness. My job is to sell an experience.
DEBBI FIELDS

A complaining customer is
a valuable commodity.
RICK SEGEL

More business is lost every year though
neglect than through any other cause.
ROSE F. KENNEDY

To open a shop is easy,
to keep it open is an art.
CHINESE PROVERB

A satisfied customer is the best business
strategy of all.
MICHAEL LEBOEUF

The competitor to be feared is the one who never bothers about you at all, but goes on making his own business better all of the time.

HENRY FORD

Touch your customer,
and you're halfway there.

ESTÈE LAUDER

Success is simple. Do what's right, the right way, at the right time.

ARNOLD H. GLASGOW

As important as we think we are at work, there is always someone who can replace us.

RICK SEGEL

If you knew the mule were blind would you
not load the wagon?

RICK SEGEL

No matter what your product is, you are
ultimately in the education business. Your
customers need to be constantly educated
about the many advantages of doing
business with you, trained to use your
products more effectively, and taught
how to make never-ending improvement
in their lives.

ROBERT ALLEN

An organization's ability to learn, and
translate that learning into action rapidly, is
the ultimate competitive advantage.

JACK WELCH

People are definitely a company's greatest asset. It doesn't make any difference whether the product is cars or cosmetics. A company is only as good as the people it keeps.

MARY KAY ASH

In the business world, the rearview mirror is always clearer than the windshield.

WARREN BUFFETT

If the buck stops at the top where does it start?

RICK SEGEL

Should you find yourself in a chronically leaking boat, energy devoted to changing vessels is likely to be more productive than energy devoted to patching leaks.

WARREN BUFFETT

Advertising is totally unnecessary. Unless
you hope to make money.
JEF I. RICHARDS

There is room for bulls and bears in the
marketplace, but pigs get slaughtered.
ANONYMOUS

In business as in life, sometimes bad things
happen to good people, and sometimes
good things happen to bad people. But over
time, if you play long enough, everybody
gets what he deserves . . . good and bad.
JEFFREY IMMEL

Customers love to buy, but hate to be sold.
ANONYMOUS (AND RICK SEGEL!)

The golden rule for every businessman is this: 'Put yourself in your customer's place.'
ORISON SWETT MARDEN

In the business world, everyone is paid in two coins: cash and experience. Take the experience first; the cash will come later.
HAROLD GENEEN

Wise are those who learn that the bottom line doesn't always have to be their top priority.
WILLIAM ARTHUR WARD

I don't look to jump over 7-foot bars; I look around for 1-foot bars that I can step over.
WARREN BUFFETT

They say a year in the Internet business is like a dog year . . . equivalent to seven years in a regular person's life. In other words, it's evolving fast and faster.

VINTON CERF

One who stops advertising to save money would stop a clock to save time.

HENRY FORD

If you a make a sale you make a living.
If you make an investment of time
and good service in a customer,
you can make a fortune.

JIM ROHN

Sell the sizzle, not the steak.

ANONYMOUS

If a product isn't selling, I want to get it out of there because it's taking up space that can be devoted to another part of my line that moves. Besides, having a product languish on the shelves doesn't do much for our image.
NORMAN MELNICK

I violated the Noah rule: Predicting rain doesn't count; building arks does.
WARREN BUFFETT

Our business in life is not to get ahead of others, but to get ahead of ourselves—to break our own records, to outstrip our yesterday by our today.
STEWART B. JOHNSON

An educated consumer is our best customer.
SYMS ADVERTISEMENT

Too many people think only of their own profit. But business opportunity seldom knocks on the door of self-centered people. No customer ever goes to a store merely to please the storekeeper.
DEBBI FIELDS

Business is a combination of war and sport.
ANDRÈ MAUROIS

Whether it's Google or Apple or free software, we've got some fantastic competitors and it keeps us on our toes.
BILL GATES

All lasting business is built on friendship.
Business is in itself a power.
GARET GARRETT

Good ideas are not adopted automatically.
They must be driven into practice with
courageous patience.
HYMAN RICKOVER

As soon as everyone is on the bandwagon
with one idea, a leader should be working
on the next one.
ROGER ENRICO

In business, the competition will bite you if
you keep running; if you stand still, they
will swallow you.
WILLIAM KNUDSEN, JR.

We see our customers as invited guests to a party, and we are the hosts. It's our job every day to make every important aspect of the customer experience a little bit better.

JEFF BEZOS

Don't bring your need to the marketplace, bring your skill. If you don't feel well, tell your doctor, but not the marketplace. If you need money, go to your bank, but not the marketplace.

JIM ROHN

Business is more exciting than any game.

LORD BEAVERBROOK

It takes more than capital to swing business.
You've got to have the A. I. D. degree to get
by—Advertising, Initiative, and Dynamics.
REN MULFORD JR.

Success in business requires training and
discipline and hard work. But if you're not
frightened by these things, the opportunities
are just as great today as they ever were.
DAVID ROCKEFELLER

If you did not look after today's business
then you might as well forget about
tomorrow.
ISAAC MOPHATLANE

Being able to touch so many people through my businesses and to make money while doing it, is a huge blessing.
MAGIC JOHNSON

In all realms of life it takes courage to stretch your limits, express your power, and fulfill your potential. It's no different in the financial realm.
SUZE ORMAN

I have found no greater satisfaction than achieving success through honest dealing and strict adherence to the view that, for you to gain, those you deal with should gain as well.
ALAN GREENSPAN

In business, I've discovered that my purpose
is to do my best to my utmost ability every
day. That's my standard. I learned early in
my life that I had high standards.
DONALD TRUMP

To be successful, you have to have your
heart in your business, and your business in
your heart.
THOMAS WATSON, SR.

The absolute fundamental aim is to make
money out of satisfying customers.
JOHN EGAN

Hire character. Train skill.
PETER SCHUTZ

"

My Favorite Business Quotes

My father taught me always to do
more than you get paid for as
an investment in your future.
JIM ROHN

You can fool all the people all the time if the
advertising is right and the budget is big
enough.
JOSEPH E. LEVINE

The NBA is never just a business. It's always
business. It's always personal. All good
businesses are personal. The best businesses
are very personal.
MARK CUBAN

The first rule of any technology used in a business is that automation applied to an efficient operation will magnify the efficiency. The second is that automation applied to an inefficient operation will magnify the inefficiency.

BILL GATES

Let's be honest. There's not a business anywhere that is without problems. Business is complicated and imperfect. Every business everywhere is staffed with imperfect human beings and exists by providing a product or service to other imperfect human beings.

BOB PARSONS

Carpe per diem—seize the check.

ROBIN WILLIAMS

I don't pay good wages because I have a lot of money; I have a lot of money because I pay good wages.

ROBERT BOSCH

You're most unhappy customers are your greatest source of learning.

BILL GATES

For all of its faults, it gives most hardworking people a chance to improve themselves economically, even as the deck is stacked in favor of the privileged few. Here are the choices most of us face in such a system: Get bitter or get busy.

BILL O' REILLY, ON CAPITALISM

Don't just let your business or your job
make something for you, let it make
something of you.

JIM ROHN

There is no business like show business. But
there are several like accounting.

DAVID LETTERMAN

People are best convinced by things they
themself discover.

BEN FRANKLIN

As iron sharpens iron,
so one man sharpens another.

PROVERBS 27:17

Somebody once said that in looking for
people to hire, you look for three qualities:
integrity, intelligence, and energy.
And if they don't have the first,
the other two will kill you.
WARREN BUFFETT

Those who say it cannot be done, should
not interrupt the person doing it.
CHINESE PROVERB

Lead and inspire people. Don't try to
manage and manipulate people. Inventories
can be managed but people must be lead.
ROSS PEROT

Everyone lives by selling something.
ROBERT LOUIS STEVENSON

Nobody talks about entrepreneurship as survival, but that's exactly what it is and what nurtures creative thinking. Running that first shop taught me business is not financial science, it's about trading: buying and selling.
ANITA RODDICK

If you go to work on your goals, your goals will go to work on you. If you go to work on your plan, your plan will go to work on you. Whatever good things we build end up building us.
JIM ROHN

To succeed in business, to reach the top, an individual must know all it is possible to know about that business.
J. PAUL GETTY

You don't close a sale, you open a
relationship if you want to build a long-
term, successful enterprise.

PATRICIA FRIPP

Whenever an individual or a business
decides that success has been attained,
progress stops.

THOMAS J. WATSON JR.

Every sale has five basic obstacles: no need,
no money, no hurry, no desire, no trust.

ZIG ZIGLAR

A mediocre idea that generates enthusiasm
will go further than a great idea
that inspires no one.

MARY KAY ASH

And old Dave, he'd go up to his room,
y'understand, put on his green velvet
slippers—I'll never forget—and pick up his
phone and call the buyers, and without
leaving his room, at the age of eighty-four,
he made his living. And when I saw that,
I realized that selling was the greatest career
a man could want.
ARTHUR MILLER, *DEATH OF A SALESMAN*

Sales are contingent upon the attitude of the
salesman, not the attitude of the prospect.
WILLIAM CLEMENT STONE

Catch a man a fish, and you can sell it to
him. Teach a man to fish, and you ruin a
wonderful business opportunity.
KARL MARX

On any given Monday I am one sale closer
and one idea away from being a millionaire.
LARRY D. TURNER

A smart salesperson listens
to emotions not facts.
ANONYMOUS

It's just called 'The Bible' now.
We dropped the word 'Holy' to give it a
more mass-market appeal.
EDITOR, HODDER & STOUGHTON

It used to be that people needed products
to survive. Now products need people
to survive.
NICHOLAS JOHNSON

Business opportunities are like buses, there's always another one coming.
RICHARD BRANSON

Most people think selling is the same as talking. But the most effective salespeople know that listening is the most important part of their job.
ROY BARTELL

If you work just for money, you'll never make it. But if you love what you are doing, and always put the customer first, success will be yours.
RAY KROC

I have never worked a day in my life without selling. If I believe in something, I sell it, and I sell it hard.
ESTÉE LAUDER

It's not the employer who pays the wages. Employers only handle the money. It's the customer who pays the wages.
HENRY FORD

One good customer well taken care of could be more valuable than $10,000 worth of advertising.
JIM ROHN

Religion and business are a dangerous combination.
RICK SEGEL

The critical ingredient is getting off your butt and doing something. It's as simple as that. A lot of people have ideas, but there are few who decide to do something about them now. Not tomorrow. Not next week. But today. The true entrepreneur is a doer, not a dreamer.

NOLAN BUSHNELL

My son is now an 'entrepreneur.' That's what you're called when you don't have a job.

TED TURNER

Leadership is the art of getting someone else to do something you want done because he wants to do it.

DWIGHT D. EISENHOWER

If it really was a no-brainer to make it
on your own in business there'd be millions
of no-brained, harebrained, and otherwise
dubiously-brained individuals quitting
their day jobs and hanging out their
own shingles. Nobody would be left
to round out the workforce
and execute the business plan.
BILL RANCIC

A man should never neglect his family for
business.
WALT DISNEY

Well, you know, I was a human being before
I became a businessman.
GEORGE SOROS

Long-range planning works best
in the short term.
DOUG EVELYN

A business has to be involving, it has to be
fun, and it has to exercise your creative
instincts.
RICHARD BRANSON

The entrepreneur always searches for
change, responds to it, and exploits it as an
opportunity.
PETER F. DRUCKER

The first one gets the oyster
the second gets the shell.
ANDREW CARNEGIE

"

No enterprise can exist for itself alone. It ministers to some great need, it performs some great service, not for itself, but for others…or failing therein, it ceases to be profitable and ceases to exist.

CALVIN COOLIDGE

Industry is the soul of business and the keystone of prosperity.

CHARLES DICKENS

The 4% Rule:
4% of all of the people you deal with belong to the PLO.
Pushy, Loud and Obnoxious…
But the other 96% are OK.

RICK SEGEL

You need to be aware of what others are doing, applaud their efforts, acknowledge their successes, and encourage them in their pursuits. When we all help one another, everybody wins.
JIM STOVALL

Who likes not his business, his business likes not him.
WILLIAM HAZLITT

The new source of power is not money in the hands of a few, but information in the hands of many.
JOHN NAISBITT

The man who will use his skill and
constructive imagination to see how much
he can give for a dollar, instead of how little
he can give for a dollar, is bound to succeed.
HENRY FORD

It's through curiosity and looking at
opportunities in new ways that we've always
mapped our path at Dell. There's always an
opportunity to make a difference.
MICHAEL DELL

Management is nothing more than
motivating other people.
LEE IACOCCA

A shopkeeper is a CEO without the glory.
RICK SEGEL

Statistics suggest that when customers complain, business owners and managers ought to get excited about it. The complaining customer represents a huge opportunity for more business.
ZIG ZIGLAR

The best executive is the one who has sense enough to pick good men to do what he wants done, and self-restraint to keep from meddling with them while they do it.
THEODORE ROOSEVELT

In the end, all business operations can be reduced to three words: people, product and profits. Unless you've got a good team, you can't do much with the other two.
LEE IACOCCA

Everybody makes business mistakes. I mean, I take the responsibility, and I did. I was the captain of the ship and I took that responsibility.

ALAN BOND

A brand without a signature line is a missed opportunity.

RICK SEGEL

The gambling known as business looks with austere disfavor upon the business known as gambling.

ALDUS MANUTIUS

Celebrate what you want to see more of.

TOM PETERS

Charge less, but charge. Otherwise, you will not be taken seriously, and you do your fellow artists no favours if you undercut the market.

ELIZABETH ASTON

The most successful businessman is the man who holds onto the old just as long as it is good, and grabs the new just as soon as it is better.

LEE IACOCCA

We are always saying to ourselves…we have to innovate. We've got to come up with that breakthrough. In fact, the way software works, so long as you are using your existing software you don't pay us anything at all. So we're only paid for breakthroughs.

BILL GATES

Innovation distinguishes between a leader
and a follower.
STEVE JOBS

A fish goes after the bait,
not the hook.
ANONYMOUS

Control your business or it will control you.
RICK SEGEL

Sign : Tipping is sexy.

Sign: If you like our service tell others. If you don't tell us.

Are you customers saying wow?
TOM PETERS

Making your business like a family is NOT the best role model. Families argue, disagree, complain, and treat each other poorly, so why is this a good thing?
RICK SEGEL

Money is a very delicate thing.
BEN HURVITZ

Brand equity is the amount
of extra money someone is willing to pay
for the exact same item.

RICK SEGEL

Define your business goals clearly so that
others can see them as you do.

GEORGE BURNS

There are a lot of things that go into creating
success. I don't like to do just the things I
like to do. I like to do things that cause the
company to succeed. I don't spend a lot of
time doing my favorite activities.

MICHAEL DELL

Everything Else

"

Too much of a good thing
is wonderful.

MAE WEST

About the time we think we can make ends
meet, somebody moves the ends.
HERBERT HOOVER

Do not remove a fly from your friend's
forehead with a hatchet.
CHINESE PROVERB

Adrenaline is a powerful tool that can rarely
be trained.
RICK SEGEL

I hear and I forget. I see and I remember.
I do and I understand.
CONFUCIUS

People who say they sleep like a baby
usually don't have one.
LEO J. BURKE

To err is human, but to really foul things up
requires a computer.
FARMERS' ALMANAC, 1978

Folks from the South may talk slowly . . .
but they listen just as fast.
RICK SEGEL

When I took office, only high energy
physicists had ever heard of what is called
the Worldwide Web . . .
Now even my cat has its own page.
BILL CLINTON

Forgive your enemies,
but never forget their names.
JOHN F. KENNEDY

Make sure you have finished speaking before
your audience has finished listening.
DOROTHY SARNOFF

The difference between love and hate is such
a thin line.
RICK SEGEL

No matter how rich you become,
how famous or powerful, when you die
the size of your funeral will still pretty much
depend on the weather.
MICHAEL PRITCHARD

Reading is to the mind
what exercise is to the body.
SIR RICHARD STEELE

The only way to entertain some folks
is to listen to them.
KIN HUBBARD

The exciting difference is the difference.
RICK SEGEL

Take rest; a field that has rested
gives a bountiful crop.
OVID

A friend's eye is a good mirror.
CELTIC PROVERB

It's never just a game when you're winning.
GEORGE CARLIN

Be careful about reading health books.
You may die of a misprint.
MARK TWAIN

Being different is as bad as it is good.
RICK SEGEL

An ignorant person is one who doesn't know
what you have just found out.
WILL ROGERS

Advice is what we ask for when we already
know the answer but wish we didn't.
ERICA JONG

Not asking dumb questions is dumb.
RICK SEGEL

Cheers to a new year and another chance for
us to get it right.
OPRAH WINFREY

Time is like money, the less we have of it to
spare the further we make it go.
JOSH BILLINGS

My Favorite Business Quotes

Life is too complicated not to be orderly.
MARTHA STEWART

Every phrase has two meanings.
RICK SEGEL

We are currently not planning on
conquering the world.
SERGEY BRIN

Sex is important.
RICK SEGEL

The winner is the chef who takes
the same ingredients as everyone else and
produces the best results.
EDWARD DE BONO

Culture is everything we don't have to do.
ENO'S FIRST LAW

It is OK to use the word SUCK today.
It just feels sucky saying it.
RICK SEGEL

Toto I have a feeling we are
not in Kansas anymore.
WIZARD OF OZ, JUDY GARLAND

The difference between men and woman are both more and less than we realize.
RICK SEGEL

Come back, Shane
SHANE, BRANDON DE WILDE

The smartest people can say the dumbest things. While the dumbest people can say the most profound.
RICK SEGEL

If the shoe doesn't fit must we change the foot?
GLORIA STEINEM

ACKNOWLEDGEMENTS

The first person we must thank and acknowledge is the person that spent hours doing research, spending time online, and prodding me to come up with the quote of the week that would appear in my weekly newsletter. That person is my wife, Margie Segel. She has an uncanny way of translating my ideas into workable, useful projects and products. This book is the end result of her efforts. To use a quote from the book, "It's not how many ideas you have it's how many ideas you make happen." Margie makes ideas happen. Thank you!

Next we want to thank Amy McHugh for taking the quotes from all of my newsletters and compiling them, bringing many ideas together into a real product. I also want to thank Amy for coordinating with the cover designer to capture the true spirit of the project.

Next we would like to thank Sebastian at Zitux Web & Design for capturing the essence of the project on the cover and in following up on all the little changes that have been made.

Lastly, we would like to thank our editor, Michelle Singer, from Vermont for picking up on all the things that a good editor picks up on and without changing the spirit of the project. The best editors will make countless changes that even the author can't recognize because they interpret the work the way it is intended.

Thank you!

About the Author

Rick Segel has a passion for retail! He is the ultimate business development specialist. He turns meetings into events, and events into once-in-a-lifetime memorable experiences. He has enthralled audiences in 49 states, 10 countries, and 5 continents. His best-selling *Retail Business Kit for Dummies* is just one of his respected titles. His background and expertise have allowed him to identify universally applicable secrets of success that are essential in a number of industries for making a business succeed.

Determined, passionate, entertaining and endlessly enthusiastic, Rick has been WOWing audiences and changing business owners' lives for over 20 years.

That's the accomplishment he's the proudest of.

Also by Rick Segel

The Retail Sales Bible: The Great Book of G.R.E.A.T. Selling

Retail Business Kit for Dummies

Becoming the Vendor of Choice

The Essential Online Solution: The 5-Step Formula for Small Business Success

The 5000 BEST Sale & Promotional Names & Ideas Ever Compiled

Laugh & Get Rich

How To Become The Preferred Vendor: 251 Strategies for Doing More Business with Retailers

How to Run a Sale

Retailing in the 21st Century

Awkward Moments: In Every Day Life

Powerful Promotions and Sensational Sales

Retail Business Kit for Dummies 2nd edition

Open to Thrive Merchandise Control System and Sales Register

Million Dollar Advertising on a Shoestring Budget: Ways to Increase Your Advertising Exposure While Decreasing the Amount of Dollars Spent

WOW Them Into Your Store...The Art and Science of Creating Powerful Promotions and Sensational Sales